DREAM OF ME AS WATER

DREAM
OF ME
AS
WATER

POEMS
DAVID LY

Palimpsest Press
1171 Eastlawn Ave.
Windsor, Ontario. N8S 3J1
www.palimpsestpress.ca

Printed and bound in Canada
Cover design and book typography by Ellie Hastings
Edited by Jim Johnstone
Author Photo by Joy Gyamfi

Palimpsest Press would like to thank the Canada Council for the Arts
and the Ontario Arts Council for their support of our publishing
program. We also acknowledge the assistance of the Government of
Ontario through the Ontario Book Publishing Tax Credit.

Anstruther Books

LIBRARY AND ARCHIVES CANADA CATALOGUING IN PUBLICATION

TITLE: Dream of me as water : poems / David Ly.
NAMES: Ly, David, author.
IDENTIFIERS: Canadiana (print) 20220278512
             Canadiana (ebook) 20220278520

ISBN 9781990293184 (SOFTCOVER)
ISBN 9781990293191 (EPUB)
ISBN 9781990293207 (PDF)
SUBJECTS: LCGFT: POETRY.
CLASSIFICATION: LCC PS8623.Y22 D74 2022 | DDC C811/.6—DC23

Table of Contents

Dream

Dream of Me

Dream of Me as Water

DREAM

Blue Passion

I used to think too much,
I used to think I felt
too much, especially
when good feelings
spread and I couldn't control
how much, how fast

as when I was gifted
a blue passion flower
plant and the potential
of nurturing something
sweet rooted in my mind

and bloomed all over
my cerebrum, in the grooves
of my brain. White petals
flushed with pink
unfurled to reveal a crown
of purple and blue filaments

where I used to think
I felt too much, especially
when good feelings
spread and I couldn't control
how much, how fast

Autobiography as a Thunderstorm

Listen to how quiet I am
after admitting that I'm afraid

of thunderstorms. It's hard
to discern hail from the rain

smacking the window
while I lie in bed thinking

of my mom mentioning
that my fear of rain

came from a past life
where I died as a soldier

fighting during a storm,
unable to tell the difference

between bullets and hail
hitting metal as I lost blood.

I can't fall asleep, so I head
to the couch debating

if listening to "Thunder"
by Imagine Dragons

is too on the nose for tonight.
I recall telling you that I love

windstorms (but only during
the daytime), and imagine

dragons responsible for them
when they take flight

creating gusts to remind
us that they still exist.

I'm glad you indulge
my theory, and yes, a vast

imagination is one thing
I'm glad flows in my family.

A boom is struck, brightening
my living room with a flash.

The window sounds close
to shattering, wind howls,

and hail moves bullet-like
against the glass—

memory may not be
generous for a second time

if I carry too much
of myself into the next life.

Dream

Inside the dream a boy throws himself
      into an ocean

Inside the dream water bleeds into his body's
      hollows

Inside the dream bioluminescence
      lights the ocean floor

Inside the dream the boy swims the ocean
      inside himself

Inside the dream songs are half-human
      half-serpent

Inside the dream the boy who threw himself
      into the ocean wakes

There Are Thousands of Tardigrades on the Moon. Now What?

When we're silent
        I hear the worst
possible things in my mind.
The lack of sound
             reverberates
and I prepare
to spew unnecessarily
             harsh words, contemplate
             how being the first
             to speak could
create a vacuum
of silence
that neither of us would want

to venture into.

        So I allow the quiet
        between us to become vaster,

      a nothingness where our bodies
      are so still we would wake
        if a few droplets
          of water fell
             onto our skin.
We're intimately
aware of changes we want

      to leave on each other's worlds,

        but how to set them in motion

is alien to us.

Following the universal
aphorism that all things start small,

let's wait out the molecular moments,

           the uncomfortable reticence
that can catalyze
a chain reaction
    of meaningful exchanges.

    We can adapt together, even when
    it seems that nothing else can.

What He Saw

Almost every night, he'd insist we stargaze. Overlooking the forest, I'd stare as he tilted his head toward the sky, muttering about beauty even when it was cloudy. I always tried to see what he saw, but never did until, one night, a meteor broke through the clouds. He hardly reacted when I yelled for us to leave. Running back down the cliff, he veered off and I couldn't keep up. I kept looking for him until the sun came up. Orchids of all colours had taken root on the tree branches, even though they'd never been seen in the area before. I followed and they became denser until I stood in the crater where the meteorite landed. He was sitting up against it, hands in his lap, head looking down. I slid to my knees to cradle him and his body fell limp into my chest. Caressing his face, beautiful alien-like petals bloomed from his half-closed eyes.

Love
after "Evil"

knows that time apart is time spent together

Love is waiting

Love is the choke you experience

when speaking about what you need

not what you think you'd like to hear

Love is the terror you're ready to confront

Love tastes like salt

it hurts and holds you

Love swims with, and often times

against the current

despite your wildest imaginings

Love is never doing what you think it is

Love can be left alone

you can be left alone, Love

Love can't be blamed

for everything, for everything, for everything

Love is a beast you're ready to look in the eye

Love doesn't have to be

everything, not everything can be loved

Love
apologizes
disappoints
apologizes
forgives
disappoints
forgives
apologizes
forever

Love speaks words that shake you

to your foundation

Love is the fear you hear in your own voice

when it says *I'm ready*

Hello, Worry

Apparently it can help
to picture a cloud
passing across the sky.
With my eyes closed
I allow one to keep
drifting beyond
my field of vision—
the harder I force it
to move, the slower
it seems to advance.
Still, I never take
my eyes off of it
or forget about
the clear sky
that's always there
always there

I Want to Believe in Essential Oils

Lana Del Rey croons through
a "Made For You" Spotify playlist
about having cinnamon
in her teeth. I swallow an urge
to cry that comes from nowhere,
put five drops of lavender
and bergamot orange into a black
teardrop-shaped diffuser
and use a peppermint roll-on stick
around my temples in anticipation
of a headache. I want to believe
these oils can soothe me,
but all I feel is a craving
for someone, something sweet,
or maybe cherry-flavoured
Hubba Bubba between my teeth.

Godzilla (2014)

brings a tsunami
                    as he swims,
                    shark-like,

    shaking theatre walls
                    with a roar
that takes me
            back to childhood,
            mimicking the King
    of the Monsters
                    when he stomped
Ghidorah's three golden necks.

        Now, he rises from the water
        crashing through
                Golden Gate Bridge,
                        missiles exploding,

        fire engulfing gills
        that were redesigned
        to have his existence
                be more logical
                in *our* universe,
    to help him breathe underwater.

                        Godzilla:
                    form altered
        when nobody had to change
you—

you would have always
been understood
                even when the nuances
        of how you exist
    were your own.

Lucifer Flowers

Sneaking up on the past from behind
I grab the silver ram horns curling
from its head and yank until I hear
a scream, boyish and afraid,
louder as I kick the back of its knees
and it buckles into the mud,
voice drowning, its three-fingered
claws scratching at my eyes,
eventually surrendering, trembling
on all fours and whimpering
until I tighten my grip and twist
and snap time's neck, its body
limply smacking the mud, Lucifer
flowers beginning to wilt around us.

To Each Their Own (Arm of a Giant Pacific Octopus)

After days of not looking
so well
you detach
by some kind of science,

writhe away
and magically grow
a whole body
of newfound limbs.

Happier that you're free
moving with more you
I reach out
enviously stretching

my body
into what turns
out to be a broken
glass bottle.

How do I heal?
I'm not brave enough
to break away
and flourish by myself,

but maybe without you
I can nurture my own
form of courage,
however it may look.

Follow

I was once told to walk in the direction moss grows
to reach civilization. Or was it that I could tell
which way the sun rises depending on the side
moss roots on boulders and trees? We've been lost
in these woods for longer than I want to admit.
If we keep walking, I'll know not to trust
myself to lead us, but will you still want to follow
once the forest roots inside of me?

Waking Alone in Another Dream
after "Walking Together at the End of the World"

The water ripples and I jolt
                              awake on my back.
            Two full green moons stare down at me.

I'm alone when we're together
                      holding hands, walking
            across a liquid landscape.

                              On my own, my imagination
                  spins as many possibilities as there are
            constellations in this unfamiliar sky

but I still can't explain why you can't exit
this dream with me.

      We shared unspoken promises
                  to never be apart,

but this is what happens when you believe
                              in mythical men and walk with them

at the end of the world. The moons are drowning
            in approaching sunshine and I'm still breathing—

                  the brighter it gets,
            the more clicks and whistles
                  come from beneath the water.

                  I bob up and down
as the sea moves around me, its muscular hands

holding
> my arms and neck, caressing

before releasing,
> taking its haunted songs back to the deep.

Without you, I can actually stay
afloat, even if it's just in another dream.

Future Excavation

Enter "how to become a paleontologist" and David
enters his first dig site in an alternate timeline.

There he unearths dramatically long vertebrae
belonging to a Spinosaurus that swam the waterways
of long-gone mangrove forests, stalking unsuspecting aquatic prey
while the iconic sail on its back broke the water's surface.

This David isn't bad with science like I am.
Instead of using imagination to craft poems

                    he poured it into hypotheses about functions
             and peculiar features discovered in prehistoric
organisms that wander onto the page from time to time.
He was brave enough to do more than just dream of another reality

                    confidence evolved into a form of expression
but positing alternate futures is like speculating about the past—
nobody knows how Spinosaurus behaved but it would be wonderful
to witness what their lives were like even for a moment.

DREAM OF ME

Good Morning, Stress

I ask Google why I'm angry in my dreams.
The featured result suggests that I may be attuned
to frustration or agitation. While true to a degree,
I hide the frequency at which stress flows
in my waking reality, the muscles that bear my body.

Here, dreams come from the dread of learning
that sometime in the next 4.5 billion years
the Andromeda–Milky Way collision is inevitable.
I do RMT-prescribed stretches until my back
begins to burn, then sit back down to watch

Neil deGrasse Tyson explain how Earth's night
sky might look when it collapses. The galaxy
as we know it won't be the same, habitability
on Earth will be unlikely, and my tension increases
into a spasm I doubt stretching can remedy.

On screen, technicolour nebulae extend through
the universe. I ask Google: what nebula is in Scorpius?
Maybe it's the reason why my stress's gravity
is an escapable force. The constellation's Butterfly
Nebula could explain my frequent states of agitation.

If not, at least my lepitopterophobia. Earth's image
on T.V. begins to blur, and Neil's voice speaks
directly to me: "Andromeda is only minutes away
from our Milky Way now." I become more annoyed
by the second that life will end before I've conquered

my fears, especially the possibility of anger becoming
a larger part of who I am. The last thing I see
is a livestream of the collision, its colourful explosion
jolting me awake with a misshapen knot
in my neck from sleeping, contorted in dream.

While Watching *Life in Color with David Attenborough*

I've been trying to double-tap images
of reptiles and aquascaping designs
so that Instagram's algorithm will stop

flooding my search screen with photos
of impossibly attractive men.
I pray it works, sending heart

emojis to beautiful betta tanks,
though I still can't help but wonder
if those two shirtless men snapped

laughing, getting along while working
out was genuine or if it was done
for the likes I gave, only seeing one side

of things, like how two yellow damselfish
are actually completely different species
when viewed through an ultraviolet camera

revealing different markings on their scales
appearing to play with one another
when they could just want their own space.

Questioning my Fears

Are you as exhausted as I am?

Which of you will be with me the longest?

Will you lay awake with me?

How can we learn to trust one another?

Where do you lead?

Is there such a thing as trust?

Which of you can I ignore the longest?

Do you enjoy my company
as much as I enjoy yours?

Is it okay to write you like this, without any restrictions?

Will you keep me away from harm?

Dream of Me

A lonesome blue halfmoon
betta swims above me
as I approach a mirror of water—heart beating
in my throat, sweat beading on my brow—
but my reflection
doesn't move. The fish darts over
my shoulder, flaring out its gill flaps,
tail wide, body thrashing,
trying to evoke a reaction.
I want to run away
but instead scream, sending
ripples through the ceiling,
the betta's fins tearing,
violently whipping around itself
as I wake alone.

Seas of Origin

He tells himself that he doesn't need to reference
race, racism, or queerness in his poems,
yet spirals in guilt when he wishes to simply
recount feeling at ease after re-arranging
the décor in his fish tank, his possibly intuitive
compulsion to use fake plants in aquariums
as a metaphor for artificial realities created
around the themes lurks under the surface

of his words. Maybe it's natural for him to return
to the three seas where his existence is rooted
from time to time, pulled back to write about
facets of identity while trying to imagine how else
he can be seen, like a freshwater eel instinctually
finding its way to the Sargasso Sea in order to spawn,
the larvae metamorphosizing so they can return
to rivers before they yearn for their sea of origin.

Conducting Myself

Maybe I'm not used to being alone

or feeling content by myself.

Maybe that's exactly what I need—

I want to be the ocean

and the lightning that could

strike it at any moment.

Demons

I want to know
which I want
to know which
of my demons
should run
which of my
demons should
run free
to know which
of my demons
will run
free and come
back to me

I Want to Believe in Healing Crystals

I'm looking to feel better
on a budget, picking up
and putting down
healing crystals one after
the other, weighing
my lack of belief
against how badly I want
to love myself.
Maybe with rose quartz,
tinted when Aphrodite's
blood spilled onto stone?
But if I were a goddess,
would I help those
who go looking for it
on a bargain table: 40% off
a selection of methods
to manifest protection
and purification?
Maybe. It would depend
on the sales, and whether
or not I'd get a cut.

Devonian

If I could go back and change
one thing to prevent myself
from walking by your side
while you gave somebody else

your intense affection
I don't think anything would work.
Ever since that fish propped itself up
on sturdy bones 375 million years ago,

it led to other creatures, other steps
that made way for me to walk
with you. At the time, wanting
us to work was instinctual:

like pushing a primitive lung
-like organ to breathe
for as long as it could out of water.
But when I acknowledged

that you evolved into something
I couldn't stand by, I discovered
I was still able to move without you,
continue walking and breathing

"How I Feel Is Okay"

It's the little things

                                    you whisper

hoping the future

                                    isn't a fish

fighting its own

                                    reflection

Scorpio, The Water Sign

I remember the first
time I noticed
the ocean on fire

in a meme
captioned:
Scorpio as a water sign.

I'd never felt
more seen

so I sent it to you
for a laugh,

when all I wanted
to do was cry
that whole week.

There's something
about checking
horoscopes
on Instagram,

something
helpful about
strangers

weighing in on emotion

when a cosmic
explanation
    for why I am
    the way I am

    allows me to
        breathe
while the ocean's
on fire.

Ocean Boy

At the bottom of an ocean concealed by ice
a long muscular tail wraps itself around a pulsing orb of light

that illuminates indentations on see-through skin
where eyes might have evolved, given the opportunity.

He fantasizes about releasing a warmth he's always held,
uncurling his tail and swimming further into the cold abyss

to satisfy his curiosity for what else exists in the dark.
Or else, he could swim towards the light sensed from below,

burst through a frigid surface where cryovolcanoes ooze—
hoping his gills could handle the atmosphere.

Since the compulsion to stay in one place has started to feel
like a curse and a galaxy with billions of stars is nestled

in an "ocean world," there are new horizons for a being
with nowhere to go, trapped in a subsurface reservoir

responsible for holding unknown existences he's never
questioned, now on the edge of the knowable.

Hypothesis of Cetacean Evolution

If hoofed animals once trekked into water

eventually evolving into whales

it's arguably safe to take a few steps back

even if it gives the feeling of moving

in reverse—regression is only an illusion

so don't feel bad if you look back

before moving forward as

something unexpected and more

Cuttlefish

I don't want to be what you expect
      what you think   perceived through ink
once used to reveal a part of me   that I felt was needed
      in order to be seen.   Look at me now

stripped of all chromatophores
      unable to produce colours   to stun you
into a trance.   Don't search
      for a version of me

that's no longer here—   these lines appear
      before you can see them coming
eight arms open   to shoot out two
tentacles that pull you in
                towards a bird-like beak.

Two Truths and a Lie

I have a hard time writing
love poems that don't speak
about us in past tense.

I frequently imagine
past and present us
in futures where
we're trying to get back
to where we were.

I write with you in the room
across from me
and the space between us
tells me it's safe to keep
daydreaming through poetry.

Still

Wading into a coral reef
the pressure
  I feel dissipates
  like bubbles of CO_2

           as light webs
    my fingers

      and nudibranchs
    crawl through my hair
  kissing my scalp

    with tentacles to feed
           on the doubts I
brought to the water.

    Some can store toxins
    as defense mechanisms
stolen from creatures
           they consume

  so maybe
    if my bad thoughts
  are chemical

      reactions gone wrong
           nudibranchs
    could find
  a better use for them.

Or maybe they could
teach me
how to use
my own feelings

for protection
before I resurface
and crawl out
of the sea

wearing sadness
as tendrils
that can sting
or store anger
toxins
released whenever
I feel threatened.

DREAM OF ME AS WATER

Same Ocean

Years after being asked, where are you from?
I realized that I should've answered:
    did you know that when seawater meets
            freshwater in the ocean,
               a boundary forms
                 between them?
Though they appear to not be
mixing, it does happen, slowly
and over time: two bodies, two places
          of belonging
          coming together.
  Despite efforts to keep us
      apart, to manifest
        an individual
way of being,
the parts that make up who we are,
in a sense, are part of the same ocean.

        There is no other way to think
    about this metaphor, only a grandfather
who rigged his boat with a tractor engine
to give the family a better life,
speeding across
          water with a few
          belongings,
            carrying an ocean's
  worth of culture
that's filtered down
  generationally.

When asked where I'm from
again, I'd say that a man once
dreamed of more before turning
his gaze
towards the ocean where two
different bodies of water met
and blended until he made
landfall,
                              attempting to walk
         forward knowing that his existence
            was forever bound to two places.

Seawater

Through
I slip
through
your
fingers
like sea-
water

you hold me in a way no one else can

Ask and Answer

He asks when the octopus lost its shell and it twirls the end
of an arm, pointing back to the Mesozoic Marine Revolution

He asks when it would be okay for him to lose his carapace,
but the octopus doesn't move, waiting to feel safe

He asks why the octopus lost its shell and it melts
into a glass bottle to try and evade questioning

He asks why he needs to learn to be softer,
so the octopus emerges to embrace him

He asks how the octopus lost its shell, begging to learn,
and its skin flushes from mottled brown to yellow and orange

He asks how he can lose the ability to be so hard on himself
and the octopus wipes away his tears with the tips of its arms

Eels

I get out of bed and cough
eels into the bathroom sink
Baby eels squirm out
of bloodshot eyes
I see eels when showering
writhing in water
that falls off my body
Eels are caught in the cotton
while I towel off
Eels are stirred into tea
I sip and my tongue is an eel
Eels squirm down my throat
where they become words
I keep smashing
eels into the keyboard
to get them out of my mind
but I still feel them eeling
through the grooves of my brain
Like yesterday because yesterday
was an eel and my dream
a moray biting my hand
and pulling me into
its second set of eely jaws

I Would Love to Love

I'm re-watching *American Horror Story: Coven* and feel like it's the first time I'm introduced to the magical delights of Stevie Nicks. While her voice melodically quivers about how *Rhiannon rings like a bell through the night*, Misty Day stares in admiration, and I'm possessed by a spell that compels me to find a playlist of Stevie's greatest hits. Like any millennial, I'd like to tweet my newfound love for the singer: "I don't know if any of you have heard of her…" but before sending the tweet, my thumb hovers just in case there's something that's escaped my knowledge. I play her songs with the lyrics open on my laptop as if singing from a grimoire to feel good. *Rhiannon rings like a bell through the night* and I would love to love her without the possible terror of waking up to headlines or tweets guilting me for being a fan. Even if my journey with Stevie Nicks becomes a moral horror story, *Rhiannon rings like a bell through the night* and I think love can still be love, so long as we know that any love can be flawed at any moment.

Marine Snow (My Wish)

falls for several weeks

swelling in size with dead matter

on a darkening drift

toward the seafloor.

How much longer

to grow and feel

completely alive

before coming to rest?

I Want to Believe in Pink Himalayan Salt Lamps

You said you wanted nothing
to do with me, which is fair,
but here I am wondering how
to keep your dragon tree alive.

Once I read that a shady spot
with little water would suffice
(too much sunlight browns the leaves),
but maybe somehow the pink glow
from my Himalayan salt lamp

is too much. Every evening
for about two or three hours
it's on so that negative ions
can cleanse the room's energy.

When I feel it fill with the memory
of you saying *witchcraft*
then grabbing my ass,
making me lose balance
and knocking over the lamp

onto the plant, snapping
two of its leaves
into the soil (still
decomposing in the pot),

the guilt of allowing myself
to give up on you never appears
to die no matter how long
I keep the salt lamp burning.

Coelacanth

Oceanside, I haul my net,
reel and reel
until the present thrashes

its prehistoric fins
and stares up at me
asking

how did you forget
that I was
always here?

I've cast my net
countless times trying
to catch

the promise
of what lies
ahead

but a living fossil
mesmerizes
me in this moment

until I cut
time free
dive in

and swim
for as long
as possible

without a desire
to be
anywhere else

Ways to Deal with Worry

1. Write your worries on sticky notes.
   Throw them on the ground and draw a circle around them.
   Sprinkle salt onto the circle to light it on fire.

2. Start by texting, "I'm worried that…" in a message
   to yourself. Think about how sweet pecan pie is,
   and allow autofill to do the rest.

3. Leave a bottle outside during a storm
   and see how much lightning you can catch.
   When it's just about full, take a sip.
   If you're still thirsty, move on to #9.

4. Uninstall Twitter.

5. Actually, just throw your phone into the circle
   with the sticky notes.

6. Put on *Our Planet* and listen to David Attenborough
   explain how sea grass absorbs carbon dioxide
   to counteract the warming of shallow seas,
   and then sulk about the death of the Earth.

7. Lay in bed and listen to Greta Svabo Bech;
   how she pulls poetry set to Ludovico Einaudi's "Experience"
   and wonder about how you could work it into a poem.

8. Finally bathe your healing crystals in moonlight.
   Think about how they haven't made you feel better before.

9. Drink some water to see if it helps.
   If you find that you're still thirsty,
   go back and try #1 again.

10. Make a list of ten random points
    over the course of two weeks
    to get your mind off of the constant worry
    you feel for no apparent reason.

Folklore

I used to know a boy who would rage
quietly. Once, when he found
himself surrounded by wolves
he unflinchingly grabbed one by the neck
and ripped out its tongue.

                         I knew him
for too long, his anger too ingrained,
so I didn't stop him when he walked
into the forest and waded into the lake,
leaving me to whimper with the wolves.

Swamp Song

I find myself in a swamp where leaves
change before my eyes, though I never
feel the seasons' transition. Taking off
my face, I hide it in an alcove of roots
that twist up from the murky water.
Soon I hear a piano playing a slowed-down
version of a pop song I recognize,
but don't know the name of, and I start
to run, making sure to feel every rock,
the mud, the water's resistance. The faster
I go, the more likely it is that I'll never
know the name of the song, but it's not
important, especially when I encounter
the music of frogs competing to be heard,
each one believing they are louder than the next.

Tonight

                slip more
than just a finger

through
       the surface,

what's perceived

       as safe
              to satisfy
              a curiosity.

       What could
exist

in the realm
of the imaginative mind?

          Softly lit
by glowing lures

          thought
leaks

   (drop by drop)

into a disordered world.

       But tonight,
       forget

the chaos
that floods above

and plunge
in deep—

the mind never
leaks

quite quickly enough,

might as well
plunge,

plunge in deep

and breathe

Sleep Well, Doubt

10mg of melatonin popped
after missing

> Jupiter and Saturn's
> Great Conjunction

on account of a cloudy sky

It's been impossible to see beyond
the recurring image

> of "a boy under a blanket
> of shimmering, silver moths"

for the last four years

A firmer grasp of self has formed
but ideas of why

> I am who I am
> slip further away

dissolve like pills under my tongue

Remembering Black Lake

I don't remember that night
being quiet exactly. The silence
was more like a fully grown
human being painlessly bitten
by a blue-ringed octopus—
not a single cry until creatures
burst from egg sacs shrieking
and leaping towards us
as I gripped the oars in a panic.
I rowed us to shore while you
held my knee. You remember
Black Lake as the first time
we were safe together,
not as the night I had to stifle
my fear for both our sakes,
and truthfully, I wouldn't want
to remember us any other way.

Somniloquy

My boyfriend
tells me
I muttered

"not yet
it's not red enough"
in my sleep
last night.

Now that I'm awake
I have no idea

what he's talking
about.

Maybe that video
of an octopus

changing colours
as she sleeps
played

behind
my eyelids,

pastel white skin
flashing
yellow?

Apparently
                    she flushes

    when she dreams.

            I want to ask
            what she imagines,

                    if she can paint pictures

            of what she thinks happens
                    in my mind.

            When my boyfriend
            leaves

                    I hope my dreams are still
                    colourful,

allow me
to inhabit
                    any shades
                    I want,

to colour my mind

                    in ways that help me
            comprehend myself

            in the waking world.

I Only Remember Dreams When Stressed

A white peacock clicks his pearly talons
in a cacophony of Blundstones and heels
bustling through the Commercial-Broadway
SkyTrain platform on a bright winter
morning, occasionally chirping at passersby
that come close to stepping on his iridescent
train of feathers. People wait behind
the yellow line as the bird rustles through
the crowd, leaps onto the tracks, wings
thunderously flapping to soften its landing
on rusted metal. Sparks fly everywhere
and everyone ignores the bird's
trumpeting, muttering in frustration
that the train is going to be delayed again.

Wilder Spell
after "Wild Spell"

Too many men are afraid
to be tender, raw.

My love makes me fearless
with fangs and a flickering

tongue plucked from a king
cobra—surpassing

the wildness someone else
wished into me

until I was abandoned.
Nothing between us

is forbidden, too much,
too scary. Your talons

squeeze me and my pupils
dilate—grip tighter.

I want to watch you watch
me quiver.

Dream of Me as Water

Just call me friend
and I'll hold
my breath for you.
Slink back
into this cuttle-
fish lagoon,
    its neon pulses
    a warning
    to the stars
    that they will
    need to come
    down to the dark
    if the heavens
    want you back.

Stay. Lay with me
in this murk, deep
    out of sight
    from the universe.
    There is nothing
    more soothing
    than returning
    to the water
    with only
    our unyielding
    imagination
    of whatever
    we want to be,
    once we sense
    it's safe
    to re-emerge.

Notes

"There Are Thousands of Tardigrades on the Moon. Now What?" takes its title after a 2019 article on livescience.com of the same name by Mindy Weisberger.

"*Godzilla* (2014)" is titled after the 2014 Godzilla film.

"Remembering Black Lake" is a companion piece to "Memory of the Black Lake" printed in issue #92 of *Arc Poetry Magazine* and *Best Canadian Poetry 2021*.

"Love" is a response poem to "Evil" which appears in *Mythical Man*.

"Wilder Spell" is a companion piece to "Wild Spell" which appears in *Mythical Man*.

Acknowledgments

Thank you to the following publications for including previous iterations of some poems in this book:

a fine. collection, vol. 1: "I Want to Believe in Healing Crystals"

Augur Magazine, issue 4.2: "Ocean Boy"

chaudiere books blogspot, National Poetry Month 2020: "Lucifer Flowers" (published as "Caught")

Cypress, Spring 2020: "Follow" (published as "Green Man")

Heavy Feather Review's Haunted Passages feature: "Dream of Me"

the lickety-split (*@olicketyspit*), a Twitter journal, Sept. 21, 2021: "Seawater"

Not Your Best 2: Queer as Fuck, Fall 2021: "Blue Passion"

Plenitude, Fall 2019: "Wilder Spell"; Summer 2021: "Ways to Deal with Worry"

The Puritan: "Same Ocean"

SAD Mag Online, September 2021: "Eels" and "I Want to Believe in Essential Oils"

The /tɛmz/ Review, Winter 2018: "Dream of Me as Water"; Winter 2020: "Demons" and "I Want to Believe in Pink Himalayan Salt Lamps"

Train, issue 9: "I Only Remember Dreams When Stressed"

Wrongdoing Magazine, issue 1: "What He Saw"

Thank You

To Aimée, Jim, and the entire Palimpsest Press team for believing in me and my work again.

To Ellie Hastings for bringing the look of this book to life.

To Jen Sookfong Lee and Adéle Barclay for being my first readers. Thank you for the exceptionally kind words about *Dream of Me as Water*.

To Jordan Abel for selecting "Same Ocean" as the 2021 winner of the inaugural Austin Clarke Prize in Literary Excellence, administered by *The Puritan*.

To Aaron Schneider and Amy Mitchell, Founding Editors of *The /tɛmz/ Review*, for first publishing the poem "Dream of Me as Water" in their Winter 2018 issue.

To the Canada Council of the Arts and BC Arts Council for supporting this book.

To readers of *Stubble Burn* and *Mythical Man*. Thank you for sticking with me!

David Ly is the author of *Mythical Man*, which was shortlisted for the 2021 ReLit Poetry Award. He is also co-editor (with Daniel Zomparelli) of *Queer Little Nightmares: An Anthology of Monstrous Fiction and Poetry* (Arsenal Pulp Press, 2022). David's poems have appeared in publications such as *Arc Poetry Magazine, Best Canadian Poetry, PRISM International,* and *The Puritan,* where he won the inaugural Austin Clarke Prize in Literary Excellence. *Dream of Me as Water* is his sophomore poetry collection.